T0286029

WRESTLING MERCHANDISE OF THE 1990s

KEVIN WILLIAMS

AMBERLEY

First published 2022

Amberley Publishing
The Hill, Stroud
Gloucestershire, GL5 4EP

www.amberley-books.com

Copyright © Kevin Williams, 2022

The right of Kevin Williams to be identified as
the Author of this work has been asserted in
accordance with the Copyrights, Designs and
Patents Act 1988.

ISBN 978 1 3981 0720 5 (print)
ISBN 978 1 3981 0721 2 (ebook)

British Library Cataloguing in Publication Data.
A catalogue record for this book is available from
the British Library.

Origination by Amberley Publishing.
Printed in the UK.

Introduction

From the uprising in the 1980s to the limits of the late 1990s wrestling drew mass crowds worldwide, featuring all sorts of crazy matches, characters, moments and, yes, of course, merchandise. This book is here to celebrate those glory moments and hopefully it can rekindle the fond memories of pro wrestling you may have. From the Golden Era of wrestling to the Attitude Era, we celebrate the merchandise that made wrestling that bit extra special during a time of great wrestling and enjoyment.

Between 1985 to 2002 wrestling rode the crest of a wave, and in between that we celebrate the greatest of times: the 1990s. Vince McMahon's World Wrestling Federation (WWF) became the leading force in sports entertainment, while Ted Turner's World Championship Wrestling (WCW) gave good credibility to the wrestling industry, offering a fantastic alternative.

When ITV cut British wrestling from their schedule in 1988 it was left to the American stars to fill the void, and by 1990 WWF and WCW had done just that. Old British wrestling favourites Big Daddy, Giant Haystacks, Marty Jones, Johnny Saint, Mark Rollerball Rocco and Kendo Nagasaki, plus the hundreds of other British wrestling stars, had been replaced by the more muscular American 'superstars' of wrestling.

For decades British wrestling helped innovate the landscape of pro wrestling and became the antecedent for a large amount of modern wrestling's success. But what set American wrestling apart from British wrestling was their approach to the showbusiness side of things. Traditionally, Britain stuck to its grappling-style wrestling contests in bingo halls and local theatres, whereas WWF and WCW introduced celebrities and large arenas, aiming for a 'Hollywood' mentality.

At 6 feet 8 inches, 302 lbs and boasting 24-inch 'pythons' (biceps), Hulk Hogan ruled the roost for the American wrestling scene. British fans were familiar with Hogan as he starred in the film *Rocky III* as Thunderlips. His impact on wrestling and the movie industry made him a household name to millions worldwide.

It wasn't just Hogan who drew in the audience, however; Ultimate Warrior achieved similar success as world champion in 1990. And standing at 7 feet 5 inches, André the Giant added to the spectacular. Along with all the other characters and gimmicks, this turned an average wrestling show into a world-famous extravaganza.

Not forgetting the stars of the 1990s, fans were also tuning into see the 'Million Dollar Man' Ted Dibiase, 'Macho Man' Randy Savage, The Bushwhackers, 'Hacksaw' Jim Duggan, Razor Ramon, British Bulldog and the Doink the Clowns in this great era. Appealing to the kids with cartoon-like gimmicks, wrestling had moved on to the next level in the early 1990s.

WCW didn't stand still during this time. They provided fantastic wrestling shows, and being broadcast on terrestrial TV (ITV) gave them a slight advantage over their competitor. Sting, Lex Luger, Ron Simmons, Big Van Vader and Ric Flair all carried championship gold for the company, providing a comparable wrestling theme to the WWF. This proved to be a golden era for wrestling and the fans.

Wrestling hit a lull by 1994 and it wasn't until the rise of the Attitude Era of wrestling in 1996 that we see the interest return. The cartoonish early 1990s Golden Era was replaced with a more aggressive, adult theme. Pro wrestling had never seen anything like this before. Gone were the clowns and whacky tag teams, and in its place were the reckless antics of 'Stone Cold' Steve Austin, extreme wrestling matches and borderline sexually explicit storylines. The era had changed, and wrestling fans were loving every minute of it.

Surprisingly, Extreme Championship Wrestling (ECW) lifted the lid on wrestling and introduced an American audience to a more hardcore style. Like the Attitude Era, everything WWF did had mostly been seen before at ECW, but not on a global scale. When World Championship Wrestling started to broadcast at the same time as WWF on Monday nights in the States, things started to hot up between both companies. WCW, who captured the signatures of many former WWF headliners, dominated in the TV wars and in the process pushed wrestling to new heights.

Creating the New World Order (NWO) lead by Hulk Hogan, Kevin Nash and Scott Hall, WCW took wrestling into a new direction, leaving the WWF reeling from their success. ECW at the time was the third alternative; they carried on with their theme of wrestling and never looked at WCW or WWF as competition.

It took eighty-three weeks for WWF to get back on top of the business in the TV ratings, thanks to the new stars of The Rock, Mankind, Triple H and D-Generation X to name a few. The wrestling wars continued, and from 1998 WWF took control. Sadly, in 2001, both ECW and WCW were no more thanks to a buy-out from Vince McMahon.

Although pro wrestling may have changed today and the companies are no more, in this book we honour the legends who made all of this happen and remind ourselves of the great times with the wrestling merchandise of the 1990s.

This book is dedicated to my niece Ellie and nephew Zak, and a special mention goes to my sadly deceased wrestling buddy Lee Bevan as we rerun wrestling madness with the merchandise we loved.

Kick-starting this book, we head back to celebrate the rise of the Golden Era of wrestling by exhibiting these incredible action figures made by LJN for the World Wrestling Federation (WWF).

As American wrestling grew from a territorial family-run business model into a sports entertainment showbusiness style, the merchandise and the fanbase grew alongside it. Vince McMahon, owner of World Wrestling Entertainment (WWE, formerly WWF), had the idea to monopolise wrestling and, by doing so, he bought out the majority of the competition. By 1985 the WWF had moved on from being a regional New York wrestling promotion, forcing itself into a global brand attracting millions of viewers worldwide. McMahon would soon buy out the main competitor, American Wrestling Association (AWA), leaving Ted Turner's WCW as the main rival in the wrestling business. It would take until 1995 for WCW to gain notability as a serious threat to the WWF, fetching with it the 'Monday Night Wars', which was an ongoing battle between each company, each trying to outdo each other in their own peculiar way.

Simply known as 'Wrestling Superstars', the LJN action figure line commenced in 1984 and ran up until LJN's closure in 1989. Grand Toys of Canada would later produce six action figures in 1989, making room for a hugely desired series, with collectors often shedding decent money for such items.

Made of solid rubber and measuring 8 inches in height, the figures sold in great numbers and featured wrestlers from that era who were contracted to the WWF at that time. Although available in the UK, the figures had more of a presence in the American market. They were the very first action figures for the WWF and in years to come action figures and merchandise would branch out to a larger international audience than what LJN provided.

Sixty-four standard Wrestling Superstars action figures were made, with an additional six action figures receiving repaints of the original mould. In addition to this LJN produced a Bend-Ems line, which consisted of eighteen traditional moulds plus variations. Bend-Ems action figures are usually popular and are often seen in various action figure lines – Star Wars and Batman, to name a few.

LJN didn't stop there, though. They truly made use of a popular toy line, going on to make twelve thumb wrestling figures and 16-inch wrestling figures, then went on to stretch wrestlers, toy wrestling belts and, of course, wrestling rings. With the birth of WrestleMania and cable TV, pro wrestling went from a regional program to a breathtaking global extravaganza.

The 1980s was a great time for wrestling, and leading the way for the Golden Era was Terry Bollea, aka Hulk Hogan. Fresh from appearing in the movie *Rocky III*, Bollea certainly attracted crowds, selling out arena after arena. With an ultra-clean, all-American, good guy vibe, preaching to children and telling them to 'say your prayers and eat your vitamins', Hogan would soon become the pin-up boy for wrestling and, in doing so, he became a household name and a legend of the business.

Pictured here is a Hulk Hogan T-shirt dating back to 1989. One of the more popular T-shirts of the time, it features Hogan's famous red and yellow colours.

As we observe the wrestling merchandise of the 1990s, we must remember that without the correct storage none of this could have survived. This unique wrestling box measures 41 cm squared and is perfect for storing a variety of wrestling items, with wrestling figures being the number one pick.

To each side of the wrestling storage box images depict the Ultimate Warrior, Legion of Doom (Road Warriors) and The Rockers. It is unknown if other variations exist for either the WWF or WCW.

Everyone wanted to be the wrestling champion, so the WWF foam championship belts pictured here became available sometime between 1988 and 1990. The ultimate role play accessory achieved more success in the States than the UK, as they had better options to purchase.

In 1990, WWF and WCW wrestling merchandise had a huge appeal, but unfortunately the problem was getting your hands on it. This is not to say that everything was selling out immediately; the big trouble came when shops and retail failed to stock decent wrestling items.

A good portion of wrestling merchandise did find its way to UK retail, but items such as wrestling foam belts, T-shirts and magazine exclusives meant that you could only purchase via mail order catalogue. Action figures and VHS had their spot on the shop floor, but ordering via catalogue became tricky in 1990 as the majority came from overseas and even then we had custom fees.

Challenging the WWF in 1990 with their very own range of action figures was WCW. Their action figures were produced by San Francisco toy company Galoob and measured the same size (4.5–5 inches in height) as the WWF Hasbro line, but had been cast into a solid rubber form and didn't offer any spring-loaded actions or movements.

Suitable for any wrestling fan and showing similarities to the WWF figures, between the USA and the UK market forty-seven action figures featuring your favourite WCW wrestling stars reached retail. As a UK-based wrestling fan, it's interesting looking through the line. The USA had their own version of WCW Galoob action figures, while the UK had its own variations. The same moulds and wresterlers were used, the key difference between US and UK WCW Galoob action figures was the different-coloured ring attire.

After two full series, two tag team series and a UK exclusive range, that's all we see of the joyful WCW Galoob wrestling figures. WCW, for reasons unbeknown to myself, did carry on after the second series, going on to produce one final UK exclusive line, which included Dustin Rhodes, Big Josh, Sting, Lex Luger, Michael 'P.S' Hayes, Jimmy Garvin and El Gigante. Sought after by many collectors, owning an exclusive series WCW Galoob UK, mint-condition figure in its original packaging could set you in good stead as they attract serious money.

Made between 1990 to 1994, the WWF Hasbro action figure line became one of the most popular toy lines among fans and children worldwide. Even to this day there is a growing online community who cherish these wrestling figures (#HWO). Today, podcasts, websites, books and video channels dominate the talk, often attracting huge interest worldwide.

Each action figure measures approximately 4.5 inches tall and executes their own spring-loaded action move. Often figures were accompanied with accessories, such as Jake 'The Snake' Roberts' pet snake Damien, Koko B. Ware's bird Frankie, etc. The line grew popular and additional items were included for the WWF Hasbro line. Bop punch bags, wrestling grapple gear clothing, miniature Royal Rumble action figures, ride on trikes and wrestling rings all added to the fun.

In total, eleven series and two tag team series were released featuring WWF wrestlers from that time period. Mailaway action figures, prototypes, error cards and miniature figures were also included, but for the standard released figures it only lasted for four years. Sadly, as the WWF would see a downturn in the market, the action figure line would abruptly end in late 1994, leaving a much-desired green card series 11 at its finale.

I end this chapter by saying thank you to everyone who purchased my first book, *Wrestling Action Figures of the Early 1990s*. And for all of you who haven't, the full WWF Hasbro story is there for you to take a look through.

If you mentioned the word wrestling to anyone during the early 1990s the next word to roll off their lips would be Hulk Hogan. When Terry Bollea (later Hulk Hogan) made his way into pro wrestling during the summer of 1977 as the Super Destroyer nobody would expect the impact one man could have on the sport.

Over the next few years he used the ring names Terry Boulder and Stirling Golden. Then, after appearing on a talk show that included Lou Ferrigno – star of the TV show *The Incredible Hulk* – a radio host mentioned that Bollea had a larger muscle mass than Ferrigno. From then he came to be known as 'Hulk'. Upon joining Vince McMahon Snr at the WWF back in 1979, his name change from Hulk Boulder to Hulk Hogan stuck with fans, and pro wrestling hasn't looked back since.

While wrestling away from the WWF in the early 1980s, Hulk Hogan nailed the part of Thunderlips in the Rocky franchise, catapulting his success even further. Now a household name, Hogan would rejoin the WWF in 1983, where he captured the heavyweight title on five separate occasions.

The international climax of pro wrestling happened somewhere between 1987 and 1992, as huge records were broken in every aspect. Huge sell-out shows became the norm, TV channels couldn't keep up with the demand and, above all, wrestling merchandise sales were on another level. Leading the way with all of this was Hulk Hogan. There have been many unbelievable wrestlers in the industry, but one thing is certain: whether you love him or hate him, Hulk Hogan broke down all the barriers and, by doing so, he put wrestling on the map.

Hulk Rules and Python Power were two of many slogans used by Hulk Hogan. The teddy bear to the left has the famous Hulkamania trademark written in yellow, while the teddy to the right is simply known as the 'ugly Hulk Hogan' among collectors. The hats highlight the red-and-yellow ring attire colours Hulk Hogan became notorious for in his late 1980s/early 1990s period of wrestling.

From cartoon series to Hollywood films, Hulk Hogan's name covered just about everything in his time, so it's no surprise that this stationary set bears his image either. This was made by Copywrite in 1991.

Hulk Hogan was more than just a muscle-bound pro wrestler; he became the image of the sport, and with that comes responsibility. Millions of children around the world looked up to Hulk Hogan as he was portrayed as the ultra-clean, positive American who encouraged children to eat their vitamins and say their prayers. He was the ultimate hero.

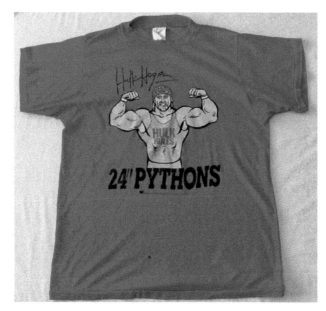

Finding wrestling T-shirts in UK shops back in the early 1990s was next to impossible; you either had to attend the live show or send away to the mail order catalogue to obtain such objects. This fine example is a US import and was found thanks to the online auction site eBay – a great place for retro wrestling goodies, but always be cautious of the import fees.

Check out the WWF logo on the T-shirt's tag – one way to identify a genuine article to a remake.

Almost everything got the 'Hulkamania' treatment. From lunch boxes to cereal packages, the Hulk Hogan branding campaign helped place WWF and wrestling on the map. As much as Hulk Hogan needed the WWF, WWF needed him too.

The muscular physique seen on the lunch box shows Hulk at his biggest. Check out the drink container too – nothing says retro more than that.

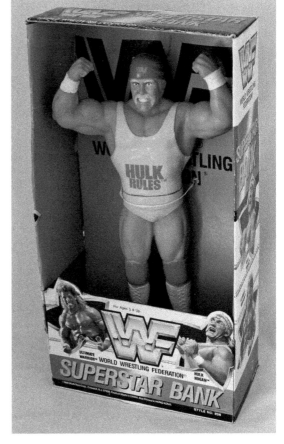

Any guesses to what this fine example of Hulk Hogan memorabilia is? It's a 'Superstar Bank' – a money box to me and you. Simply slot the coins and notes at the back of the figurine to save up your pocket money. The 'money plug' is situated just below the feet to enable you to empty the savings easily. No maker's name is visible on the box, but it is known that it was made for the WWF in 1990. It measured 15 inches in height and an Ultimate Warrior version exists too, although that is extremely hard to find.

This image shows a brand-new pair of WWF wrestling pyjamas. You have to ask yourself, 'how popular was this guy?' Well, you'd have to be high in the ranks to have your own range of wrestling pyjamas!

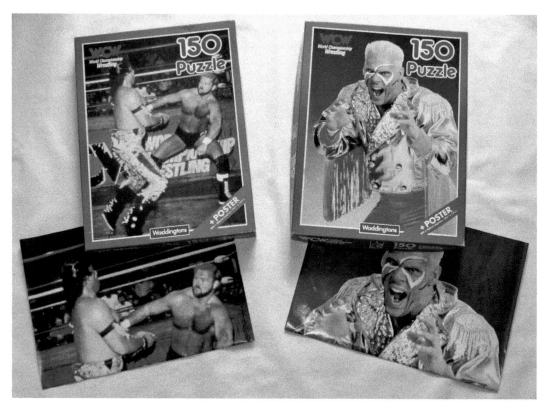

WCW were also offering a great wrestling product in the 1990s featuring Ric Flair, Sting, Barry Windham, Ron Simmons, The Fabulous Freebirds and many more top international wrestling stars. Although thought of as the second option to the WWF, the company tasted huge success in the mid- to late 1990s. Nonetheless, this didn't stop WCW from entering into the UK and European market and, in the process, producing some fantastic merchandise memorabilia.

British Satellite Broadcasting sporadically aired *WCW Power Hour* in the late 1980s to no avail, and BskyB and Eurosport did the same in the early parts of the 1990s. It took for UK terrestrial TV channel ITV to give WCW its deserved platform in and around the late 1989/early 1990 mark. With twenty-three regional broadcasting outlets for ITV, it's hard to give an exact time and date of the weekly WCW TV schedule, as each region varied their broadcasting. What most fans will remember is the regular showing of *WCW Pro Wrestling* on ITV every Saturday afternoon, which ran until mid-1995 in this slot.

The routine for any given Saturday would be WCW wrestling, followed by *Thunder in Paradise* (an action-adventure TV series that featured many pro-wrestlers), then on occasions *Airwolf, A-Team, Incredible Hulk* or whatever else was thrown at the viewers. ITV captivated a wide audience, attracting viewers of all ages.

Though it held a presence in the UK and Europe, WCW never quite eclipsed the WWF's success. The WWF held regular UK and European tours, even going on to showcase one of their top four flagship shows at Wembley Stadium – SummerSlam 1992. WWF were savvy enough to recognise the huge European market, and WCW visited in 1992 and March 1993 to well-attended events. Not a great deal more from WCW headed this way until the later 1990s. The lack of marketing surely affected the outcome of this once great company.

As Hulk Hogan dominated the scene of the competitor, Sting lead the way for WCW. He first appeared as 'Surfer' Sting (pictured here) in the early 1990s, then reappeared in as the darker, more Gothic-looking 'Crow' Sting from 1996 onwards. Steve Borden, the man behind the face paint, became recognised as one of the main players in the industry and today he stands proud as a member of the wrestling hall of fame.

To the left of this image is a wall clock and to the right is an alarm clock – both were released in 1992.

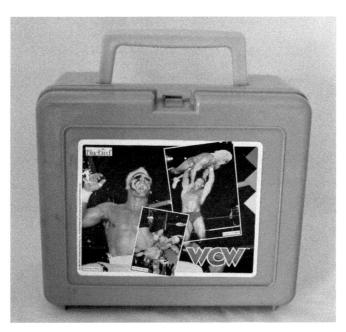

Released in 1991 by Bluebird Toys plc, this lunch box raises more questions than answers. WCW was founded in 1988 after Ted Turner purchased Jim Crockett Promotions, but the lunch box has a manufacturing date of 1981, so how did this come about? Well, putting it simply, the lunch box had been repurposed from a previous line belonging to Bluebirds Toys. Thinking quickly and taking the initiative, a sticker featuring top WCW wrestling stars was slapped on the front, making for quick readily available merchandise. Made for the UK market, this is a quirky example of early WCW merchandise.

On the left we have an original WCW Electronic Game Watch from 1991 manufactured by Systema, and to the right is a modern 2019 Wrestle Crate Vader Time wristwatch. Systema produced exceptional electronic gadgets, ranging from handheld games such as Real Ghostbusters, Gary Lineker's Football and Doctor Who to your Game and Watch-style gadgets such as the Sting version pictured here. 'Electronic fun in your pocket' became Systema's catchphrase. Although small and compact, the watch brings back many great memories.

Just some of the wonderful WCW VHS tapes available during the 1990s/early 2000s. WCW wrestling videos were much harder to find than the WWF VHS catalogue, but still they had some great releases. What is worth noting is that some WCW VHS tapes are high in value and certain ones can fetch over £50 at an online auction. WCW never branched out to DVD, making VHS the only format available for sale, driving up the interest from collectors and traders alike.

The WCW Superslam board game with top star Sting on the box display. This was made by Waddingtons in 1991. A smaller card game version of the board game was on sale at the same time. Both are easy to find, but not so easy to play.

While online streaming dominates the wrestling library we see today, the options in the 1990s was video tape or nothing else. You could catch your weekly broadcast on TV, but to rewatch over the glory moments VHS was king. Averaging £14.99 per video, you treasured every minute of every match while building up your very own video library. The quality of Blu-rays or online streaming may make videos look amateurish, but you couldn't knock the importance of VHS at the time. From your annual pay-per-view events to one-off specials, wrestling videos sold in their thousands around the world.

As wrestling figures, games, T-shirts, badges and the like have gained a larger following, video tapes have remained mostly dormant. Look out for the original VHS releases, though, because they're gradually gaining pace in the collectors' market.

Silver Vision distributed VHS for the World Wrestling Federation, providing an exceptional service in the process. If a local Woolworths, HMV, John Menzies or Virgin Megastore didn't match your VHS needs of WWF, then Silver Vision was the place to go. You would simply tick the box, fill in the order form and send it away with a cheque enclosed or, should you not own a cheque book, you could call at the nearest post office and ask for £14.99 worth of postal order as its substitute.

It may seem silly in today as everything is now at your fingertips, but back then a mail or a telephone order was the only way to proceed. And as the cheque/postal order often took over seven days to clear, you could wait up to two weeks for delivery of the order.

Every original Silver Vision/WWF product had the original blue outline to the video tape, making wrestling videos stand out as that little bit more special.

The Ultimate Warrior video pictured here was Silver Vision's highest seller, with over 90,000 copies sold in total.

Every month since 1983, the WWF provided a wrestling magazine that included the latest news, inside stories, event reviews and interviews with the talent roster. It's safe to say that the magazine was directed at children, especially as the interviews with the wrestlers were set in character.

Over the years WWE expanded its magazine appeal by offering different styles of magazines, such as poster specials, Pay-Per-View specials, Raw and Smackdown editions and one-off specials on specific wrestling stars. The magazine halted on a monthly basis in 2014 due to budget cuts. WWE occasionally releases special edition runs of magazines, usually tied to current events.

WWF magazines from the 1980s hold more value than the 1990s releases, which is due to a lower availability. Another tip is to always opt for excellent condition. Us collectors want quality.

Keeping you up to date, the WWF annual never let you down. A Christmas stocking filler for everyone, the annuals highlighted each wrestler, covering an in-depth biography plus every annual had its own quizzes and puzzles.

Every six months new catalogues displaying the latest merchandise appeared in the WWF magazine, or if you subscribed they got shoved through your letterbox. Gazing through the catalogue and having a wish list as long as your arm, in reality this could only make a child dream. The WWF knew when exactly to target you: close to Christmas or near to Easter was their calling card.

'Hindsight is a wonderful thing, if we knew then what we know now.' These words are very true. The bulk of the merchandise in the catalogues carry a heavy price today; the hardest part is tracking down the merchandise we love today.

This Hulk Hogan T-shirt was purchased on the UK and European tour of 1991. The event fared well with the UK audience and, thanks to Sky, it screened on Sky Movies. In their infancy BskyB never broadcast wrestling pay-per-view events on Sky Sports; that all began in 1992.

Here's a glimpse of just some of the wrestling titles available during the 1990s. As technology advanced, so did the gameplay. There was no better feeling than playing along as your favourite wrestler.

If you are a wrestling fan and lived through the 1990s then you have to look back and count your blessings for such a wonderful time. Enjoying the wrestling we loved and then the video gaming market's raid evolution is something not to be forgotten. From the 8-bit graphics of the NES (Nintendo Entertainment System) to the 64-bit graphics of the Nintendo 64, us '90s kids really did have the best of times and retain a lifetime of great memories.

The earlier wrestling video games were very hard to play and not as enjoyable compared to anything that came our way after 1997. With low-key graphics, minimal sound effects and the gritty kick, punch and move gameplay, the early ages of gaming were still yet to get going.

The top two games pictured became available on the Amiga, Atari ST, Commodore 64, MS-DOS, ZX Spectrum and the Amstrad CPC. The bottom one was published by LJN and featured on the original NES and Sega Master System. Check out the box damage – the younger you were when you owned these, the harder it was to look after them.

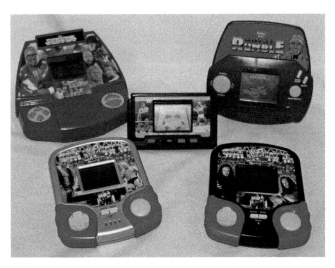

Just like the early video games of the 1990s, the handheld version didn't offer much other than sound pollution and sore thumbs. Although not the most desired of items in terms gameplay, handheld video games hold decent value in the collector's world, especially the earlier models.

This was one of the more awkward wrestling gifts to receive at Christmas. Time consuming, ultra-confusing to play and, above all, it just wasn't fun. Made by Milton Bradley, the Wrestling Challenge Game was readily available. Other international versions exist, which are known as Wrestling Championship. It's hard turning pro wrestling into a board game, and this was a stinker to play.

KidWorks made a number of fun, traditional, playable games, and here is a battery-operated action pinball game. Exactly like the real deal, this fun game parades 'Macho Man' Randy Savage as its main picture. A WWE heavyweight champion on two occasions, Randy Savage deservedly sits in WWE's hall of fame and will forever be a legend of wrestling.

Originally an 8-bit two-colour (black and green) handheld console, the Nintendo Game Boy coincided with the wrestling Golden Era of the 1990s. Over 118 million units of the Game Boy and Game Boy Color sold in its time, featuring close to 1,500 games for both consoles. A genre in itself, early Nintendo items generate huge global interest.

Pictured here are the incredible wrestling games for the Game Boy and Game Boy Color.

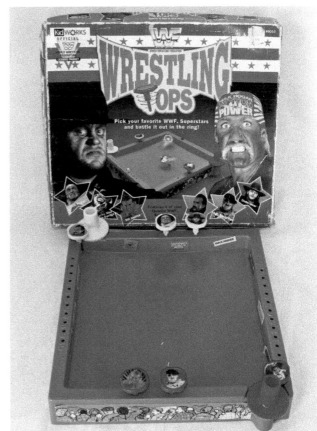

Yet another classic from KidWorks, the idea of the game is to set your wrestling top spinning and whoever lasted the longest won. Six wrestlers made up the set: three for the red team and three for the yellow team.

Sometimes the simple things are the most effective. Unfortunately, no other spinning tops wrestling games have reached us in recent times. Expect to pay close to £40 for one of these today.

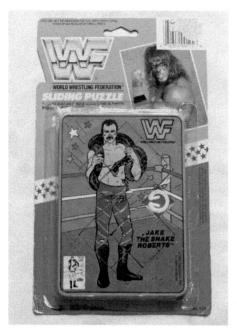

This slot-and-slide puzzle has Jake 'The Snake' Roberts as its illustration. Many other sliding square puzzles of this design exist and they are relatively easy and fun for children to play. Jake 'The Snake' Roberts had phenomenal wrestling ability and it goes to show you didn't have to be big and bulky to make it as a superstar in pro wrestling. Jake is yet again another unique wrestling talent.

Noticeably, Damien, Jake's pet snake, is sitting on Jake's shoulder in the puzzle. Fans paid good money to see Damien just as much as they did Jake. The after-match antics of throwing Damien onto an opponent really got crowds on their feet.

Mixing things up now, here we have a wallet, mini bag to store more money, playing cards and a drawing book. All items are pocket-sized and ideal to carry about. Coincidentally, the drawing book makes for an excellent autograph book.

Here's one for the children, that's for certain. An effective little package offering colouring crayons, quizzes and a colouring pad, this is the ideal rainy-day gift to keep a child occupied.

The Legion of Doom overshadow the front cover, and their arrival into the WWF is not forgotten. The super powerhouse critically acclaimed tag team were phenomenal in their heyday and fans will remember their tenacious wrestling ability. Hawk passed away in 2003 and Animal in 2020, leaving behind the Legion of Doom legacy.

The Ultimate Warrior debuted for the WWE way back in June 1987. Remembered for his muscular physique and bullish ring style, within a space of three years the Ultimate Warrior would go on to win the WWF title at WrestleMania VI.

To some the Ultimate Warrior became an absolute legend, but to others his in-ring work wasn't up to standards. Looking back some years later and that doesn't really matter. Ok, the Warrior may not have been the most technically gifted, but he could certainly get any crowd on their feet. Ask a child if they cared about the in-ring work. When the Ultimate Warrior rocked up to a show the fans went wild, and in my book he's a legend of wrestling.

Like Hulk Hogan, the Ultimate Warrior had his fair share of merchandise. Here is a boxed cup/mug made by Applause in 1990 that shows the Warrior shaking the ring ropes – a memorable trait of his.

It wasn't just Hulk Hogan and the Ultimate Warrior who only had merchandise manufactured by the WWF, but the fact is that these two drew the most money for the company so the WWF would use their trump cards to bring home the dollars. Others to have merchandise included 'Macho Man' Randy Savage, Big Bossman, Ted Dibiase, Mr Perfect, Ric Flair, the list goes on, but none were on the scale of the top two guys.

The perfect gift to make you look like a pro wrestler. Made by PAAS in the USA, this package includes six colours – metallic red, metallic blue, metallic gold, metallic, black and white. Priced at $0.99, this gloopy make-up set made for a messy encounter while attempting to dress up as your favourite superstar.

If a make-up artist held a stall at a school fate or funfair and you were like me, then instead of opting for the tiger print or the beautiful butterfly cheek you'd ask for a Legion of Doom or Ultimate Warrior makeover.

Notice the bilingual writing: this is possibly a Canadian edition, as the writing is in both French and English.

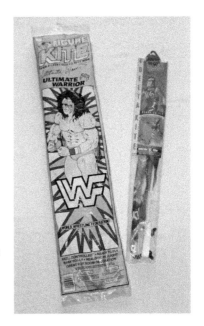

What better way to advertise your wrestling champion than wave a 4½-foot kite in the sky bearing their illustration – the Ultimate Warrior in this example. Known openly as a figure kite, the piece measures 31 inches sealed and expands to 4½ feet high by 2 feet wide when opened. The Hollywood Hogan kite measures 27 inches sealed in its original packaging and no further details are provided. Hollywood Hogan's kite comes from 1998, but both were made by the same company – Spectra Star. Other examples do exist.

Not having too many uses, this WWF briefcase is small in size and illustrates the alternative wrestling talent of 1991. Changing it up from the Hulk Hogan and Ultimate Warrior merry-go-round, this wrestling briefcase served well for carrying WWF Hasbro action figures. The keys included made it a great way to safekeep all your wrestling goodies.

The Undertaker and Bret 'the Hitman' Hart developed into headline performers, capturing the heavyweight championship on numerous occasions, and Knobbs and Sags of the Nasty Boys gained recognition as WWF and WCW tag team champions.

Even wrestling trays made it to the merchandise stalls. This was a product of Icarus Toys & Games, Bournemouth, England. Many variations to the wrestling food trays are out there and the key difference is the WWF image. Hitting retail in late 1991/early 1992, this, among other items, was supplied to the UK market.

The WWF was more than just a United States brand; they had interest in plenty of overseas countries. Take a closer look at the WWF moulding set in this chapter and you can see the item was targeted for Italy. It's uncertain to guarantee the wrestling trays were a UK exclusive, but one thing is for sure: they targeted the UK market, which was a great money spinner for both WWF and WCW.

Pictured here are three WWF watches manufactured by Nelsonic. These cartoon-style watches were released in 1991. The Jake 'The Snake' Roberts watch is a lovely addition and it's nice to see other wrestlers getting their share on the merchandise stalls.

Nelsonic had other interests away from wrestling at the same period; for example, they manufactured watches for Nintendo, Real Ghostbusters, GI Joe, Pac-Man and companies/brands of similar interest. Look closer at the wrestling watches and you will see that each watch had a moulded-on wrestler attached, which you flipped open to read the time.

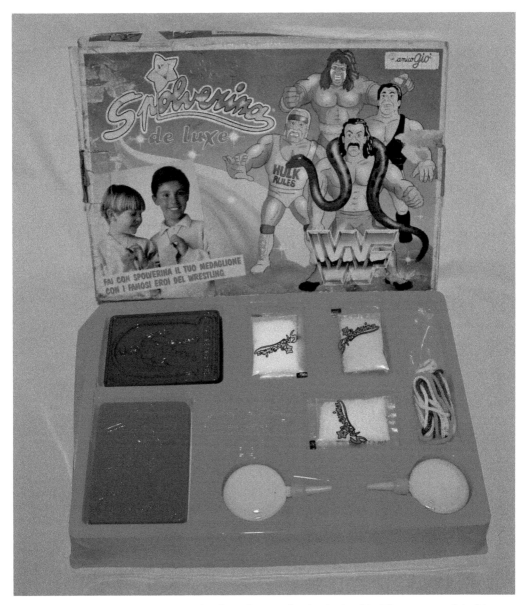

This is a moulding set made in Japan for the Italian market by Amico Gio. The purpose of the kit is to mould your very own wrestling action figure necklace. Other moulding kits were available at this time, but not for use in this way.

Each neckless is based on the WWF Hasbro style and four moulds are included. Jake Robert, Hulk Hogan, Ultimate Warrior and André the Giant make up the set. Easily thrown into the WWF Hasbro category, this is one of the most desired items on the collectors' scene.

This set of four WWF stampers was made in 1990, presenting the top four wrestlers from that time. There's nothing complicated with the design: simply dab the ink pad then press the image onto paper.

All four versions were released for retail and then given away for promotional use at fast-food restaurants such as Burger King. The promotional versions were distributed in small plastic bags – similar to what you would find today in fast-food restaurant giveaways.

The constant flow of whacky wrestling items sees the 'official' Superstar Soap Set arrive in 1991. And if the Superstar Soap Set wasn't enough, there were four to collect. There wasn't any difference in the soap; the rear of the packaging just had information bulletins of four different wrestlers.

Here we have drinking mugs, cups and flasks from 1992, featuring exceptional wrestlers from that period. The year 1992 was a pinnacle one for pro wrestling in the UK. ITV steadily increased the WCW viewing schedule, WWF was firing on all cylinders and, above all, Wembley stadium was selected to host SummerSlam 1992.

New, fresher talent found themselves in the limelight too after Hulk Hogan went on hiatus to work on his acting career. Bret 'the Hitman' Hart, Shawn Michaels, Razor Ramon and the Undertaker would emerge as the new faces of wrestling, all this while mixing it up with the old guard of Ric Flair, Randy Savage and the Ultimate Warrior.

WCW excelled with 'Ravishing' Rick Rude, Lex Luger, the Steiner Brothers and Sting at the helm. All of a sudden wrestling was cool again, but above all it became accessible. And that was thanks to ITV and satellite TV.

Gaining full media backing in the summer of 1992 placed wrestling on top of the tree. The birth of the Premier League in 1992 helped the WWF too, as more people purchased satellite to watch the football. ITV's Saturday afternoon broadcasting of *WCW Pro Wrestling* gave wrestling that extra push, making for an excellent year of pro wrestling.

Like every great rock band both WWF and WCW gave us a wide range of badges and key rings, which were mostly sold in sets or with birthday cards. From picking up items sporadically online we see a decent collect from the Golden Era of wrestling and the occasional Attitude Era addition.

It's hard to pick your favourite from this lot, especially as there are so many legends to choose from.

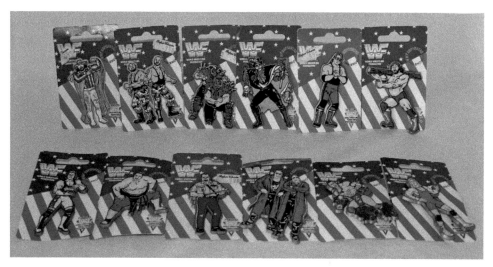

Produced in the UK, these brooches arrived in mid-1992. Measuring close to 3 inches high, they became the perfect slot machine gift. Four exclusives of Lex Luger, Razor Ramon, 'Macho Man' Randy Savage and Doink were made for the German market and today are highly sought after.

This batch of wrestling badges arrived towards the end of 1989 into 1990. Like a good portion of wrestling merchandise, these were best ordered from the mail order catalogue. Measuring up to 3 inches in height and cut intricately, the badges are bizarre in some ways but lovable in others. Definitely one for the 'different' bracket.

A rare 1992 example from the WWF. 'U.S Grade-A Prime Beef' runs along the outside, while the WWF logo and '100% tested' is seen inside. The logo often seen in magazines and the tag line for certain wrestlers is nothing more than just a logo. A muscular 'prime beef' logo bolsters the wrestler's image, demonstrating WWF's best of the best approach. Not many of these exist today, making it a rare merchandise item.

Only four wrestling stars made the cut for the popular bath salts line, which dates back to 1991. Manufactured by Grosvenor, the containers measure 12 inches in height. At this point – 1991 – Ultimate Warrior and Hulk Hogan headlined for the WWF, so it's possible the design work for the containers began in 1990. As such, why was Bret Hart chosen for the fourth wrestling bath salt when other wrestlers had more of a prominence? Did the WWF already have plans for Bret Hart to go it alone as a solo superstar? It's likely, even though in 1990 Bret Hart was competing in the tag team the Hart Foundation. Coincidentally, the Bret Hart bath salt is the scarcest of the four.

Another great piece from the CopyWrite range. CopyWrite operated out of Oxford, England, and specialised in 'stationary for bags of character'. This bumbag epitomises WWE's whacky merchandise push of 1991.

The CopyWrite range couldn't have been complete without the image of Hulk Hogan plastered all over the merchandise. Seeing as CopyWrite were based in Oxford, does this make their range a UK exclusive? Possibly not, but it is likely their products were aimed for the UK market – likewise with the wrestling food tray.

This sports bag is still sealed in its original packaging and is very difficult to find in pristine condition.

What is so unique about the swim bag pictured here is that it was found in a storage container some twenty-seven years after first being sold in 1991. The previous owner stumbled upon a huge assortment of retro wrestling merchandise in a lock-up in Portugal.

This is an event T-shirt from WrestleMania VIII. Almost every WWF and WCW pay-per-view event had its limited edition run of T-shirts, and there are collectors simply in that field alone. The most desired T-shirt memorabilia comes from the early Golden Era of wrestling and event T-shirts dating from the mid-1980s to 2002 featuring the WWF/WCW or ECW logo. There are modern T-shirts that can attract the bidders, but it's the original that gets the fans talking.

WrestleMania VIII happened on 5 April 1992 at Hoosier Dome, Indianapolis. The event featured a double main event where 'Macho Man' Randy Savaged defeated Ric Flair for the WWF championship and Hulk Hogan battled Sid Justice in his 'farewell' match.

Spotting an original from a modern reproduced example can be difficult at times and especially if you are unfamiliar with collecting wrestling T-shirts. Condition, believe it or not, can be key when it comes to originals. Often an aged T-shirt will carry some sort of wear, i.e. slight fading to the label or the colouring isn't as strong and, on occasion, smell can even play its part. Check to see if the label is legit and the seller should have a good enough background story explaining how they obtained it. Just like a rock 'n' roll band, the tour date, venue and event are printed on the back of the T-shirt.

Classic trading cards from 1989 and 1991. Both have 150 individual trading cards in each set and often reuse the famous images we have grown familiar with. The 'white boarder' sealed stickers date back to the late 1980s and can fetch good money when sealed. The 'classic blue boarder' ones are the more fashionable and are easily obtainable.

Costing just 30p per packet of eight stickers back in 1991, wrestling cards were the ideal pocket money treat. Obviously the first thing to do was burst open the wrapper and flip through the cards to reveal what wrestlers you received. Some years later and that 30p packet of trading cards is now worth close to £15 per packet.

SummerSlam 1992 will be remembered forever as the event that took the United Kingdom by storm, and it is still the highest attended UK wrestling event some twenty-nine years on. It was held at Wembley Stadium, London, on 29 August 1992, in front of a sell-out crowd of 80,355 people. The wrestling extravaganza saw Davey Boy Smith ('the British Bulldog') win the intercontinental championship from his brother-in-law, Bret 'the Hitman' Hart.

Football (soccer if you're American) has always been regarded as the leading sport of the UK, but back in 1992 WWF and wrestling stayed on par at least for a little while. In the UK football went through a transitional year by forming the brand new 'Premier League', leaving fans on the fence and uncertain of the new formation to the game. Hot with the backing of BskyB and a UK tour in 1991, people were going crazy for the WWF's product as football suffered a dip in attendance.

Parents, grandparents and mature wrestling fans couldn't get enough of the action either. Pubs and bars often hit capacity and on most occasions by 10 p.m. on a Friday evening eyes would be glued to the TV set watching *Wrestling Challenge* on Sky One.

Further to BskyB broadcasting WWF on a weekly basis, Eurosport had their own sporadic wrestling schedule, which added more engagement for wrestling fans. Then, on top of this, WCW had its own schedule with ITV (terrestrial TV), which placed wrestling high up in the rankings and gave football a run for its money. That's the impact wrestling had.

The UK's press is often associated with negative publicity, but, to give them some credit, they have always supported the wrestling scene. Pictured here are some cut outs from the 1990s era of wrestling – even the children's comic *Dandy* got in on the action.

Football, rugby, cricket, TV soaps and celebrity news dominated the majority of the press, so finding wrestling-related articles was a novelty and, in doing so, it gave a cheap insight to us fans.

Note: The 'What A Hero' article featuring Davey Boy Smith (bottom left) has been donated to his family.

The T-shirt shows an icon of British wrestling: Davey Boy Smith. Starting out aged just fifteen, Davey Boy's career took off in the mid-1980s as one half of the tag team the British Bulldogs. While tag partner Tom Billington, a legend in his own right, had to retire early due to injury, Davey Boy Smith, 'the British Bulldog', would go down in history as Britain's biggest star of that era. His biggest match was against family member Bret Hart at SummerSlam 1992, where he won the Intercontinental title for the first time.

In 1992 this T-shirt cost £11 with a £2.25 postal fee; as of 2021 expect to pay around the £100 mark. Bizarrely, that is low compared to some of the event T-shirts and merchandise of the Undertaker, Bret 'Hitman' Hart and Shawn Michaels, which generate close to the £400 mark at auction.

The tours never stopped! Since 1989 WWF/WWE has provided fans with UK wrestling events. Here's just a glimpse at some of the tour programmes from the early 1990s. It's hard to see as written in biro, but the centre programme is signed by 'Macho Man' Randy Savage.

Ticket stubs from UK events. Specific WWE/WCW and ECW ticket stubs can hold decent value. Obviously, WrestleMania and Starrcade events are the number one target for collectors. Look out for the obscure ticket stubs such as the first ever Monday Night Raw and the last ever WCW Nitro, as fans want these – more so for their collection.

More UK and European tour programmes from the WWF. This time coming from the 1993/94 time of wrestling. Notice the change in wrestling stars. No more Hulk Hogan's or Ultimate Warrior, in came Yokozuna, Crush, Razor Ramon and Shawn Michaels.

As WWF entered into a lull, the show still went on. A good portion of merchandise from this era fetches decent money as fans at the time passed on the opportunity to buy. It's strange how collectors back track to complete collections.

As great as American wrestling was there was always room for home-grown British wrestling and the 1990s gave us a mixed bag of the good, the bad and the ugly. Replacing larger arenas and stadiums with bingo halls and working men's clubs left a young child expecting more. The fanning of cigarette smoke didn't help matters either – something never seen on WWF or WCW TV.

British wrestling still had a decent amount of talent working the shows, however. The UK stars often mixed it up with the international superstars, giving a good account of themselves. On many occasions WWF, WCW or ECW wrestlers would fly over for a UK tour. It supported everyone: the promoter earned good money, the wrestler in question would receive a decent pay cheque, and the fans were happy seeing a global star on their doorstep.

If you were lucky, and like today's wrestling scene, you could be watching a relatively unknown star who in years to come turns out to be a major attraction.

The programmes here are from the late 1990s/early 2000s UK wrestling scene. Notice the gimmick Hawk of Legion of Doom image. That was common practice as many British wrestlers entered into more of a tribute act of American wrestling. Not that the British talent was faltering, it was simply logical: it drew more money.

Fresh from 1992 are the SummerSlam edition trading cards. Consisting of ninety-six cards for each set, the trading cards were released in two parts. Part one was the black trading card set, and the second part was the yellow cards. Both sold at 30p per packet of eight trading cards, and today both sets can fetch over the £60 mark if complete. What is surprising, however, is that one sealed packet alone could fetch over £10 in today's market.

Wrestling trading cards and stickers made their way into the merchandise world without fail. Year upon year fresh new batches featuring the wrestlers we adored filled newsagent stores often at the bargain price of 25p.

Present-day and collectors are still hunting down the odd card or sticker to complete sets or fill sticker albums. Cards and sticker trading have been around for centuries and it's a good hobby to have. Tracking down certain numbers can be tricky, but it's the thrill of the search that drives you forward.

The sealed cards and stickers here will never be opened – some being relatively accessible, but others are less so. The blue Series 2 stickers, WCW pink stickers and the Bret Hart centre pink stickers are by far the hardest to find out of this bunch.

The black album happened to be the first sticker album for the UK market made by Merlin for the WWF. Only 217 stickers made the cut, making way for a smooth, affordable completion of the album.

After testing the water with the black album, the blue sticker album (pictured centre) arrived in stores in late 1991. Just under 400 stickers were made for it and among them is a rare, silver, shiny WWF logo; however, bizarrely there is no room for it in the album, though it still makes for a nice addition.

Manufactured by Euroflash, WCW stickers flooded the market in 1992. Pictured to the right here, this album consists of 240 stickers and is more sporadic compared to the competition's sticker albums.

It is said the WWF saved the UK sticker album market, achieving huge popularity from their birth in late 1990. Over £80,000 of sales were reached in the first day alone, forcing shops to instantly sell out of the black album stickers. From then on stickers became big business and following that Merlin produced sticker albums for Premier League football, Power Rangers, Pokémon and *Gladiators* to name but a few.

Into 1993 and on the left is one of the tougher books to complete: the pink Bret Hart sticker album. Acquiring loose stickers is difficult now, but owning a sealed packet is on another level. The centre sticker album, the black Undertaker album, is quite the opposite to the pink sticker album: it's easily found online and stickers are available at your fingertips.

Both the pink and the black sticker albums were released in close proximity to each other in the year 1993. It's this that possibly adds to the pink sticker album's scarcity, as it was released first of the two.

To the right is the Diesel sticker album, which dates back to 1995. The album often goes under the radar and it just doesn't hold the same nostalgic worth as the others. This certainly was the time when wrestling went through its downturn. The album is the rarest of all wrestling stickers albums in the UK and finding loose stickers is extremely hard work too.

Not missing a trick, WWF jumped on the merchandise bandwagon with these four jigsaw puzzles. Each puzzle holds 200 pieces and, like cards and sticker collecting, it does have something of a therapeutic vibe surrounding it.

Made by Milton Bradley, today these can be picked up for anything between £15 to £30. You may notice that the top right Ultimate Warrior puzzle is sealed; sealed puzzles have higher value and are much harder to come by.

Selling over 49 million consoles worldwide, the Super Nintendo (SNES) is a console to be remembered. Featuring incredible games such as *Super Mario Kart*, *The Legend of Zelda: A Link to the Past*, *Street Fighter II Turbo*, *Super Metroid* and more, this great piece of machinery brings back many great memories.

Nintendo and Sega absolutely dominated the video games market in the early 1990s, both bouncing off each other and giving us everything needed for an awesome childhood. With Sega shifting 30 million Mega Drive (known as the Genesis in America) consoles, it's safe to say Nintendo ended up on top.

Photographed here is *Royal Rumble* for the SNES – an absolute classic wrestling game.

Going from the gritty, 8-bit, kick, punch and run gameplay to a 16-bit grapple wrestling game, here are some of the classic wrestling games of the early 1990s. Including wrestling theme music, more wrestling manoeuvres and better graphics, this made for a much more fun and enjoyable experience.

The aftermath of 1992 left wrestling as a hot topic. Viewing figures were still decent, fans attended events in good numbers and of course wrestling still grasped the imaginations of its audience. In 1993, WWF would move into a new direction as two of their main stars – Hulk Hogan and Ultimate Warrior – had left the company. Their replacements of Bret 'the Hitman' Hart, the Undertaker, Razor Ramon and Shawn Michaels kept the juggernaut rolling.

Mike Stock and Pete Waterman (from British song writing team Stock, Aitken and Waterman) oversaw the project of the *WrestleMania* album in 1993, which featured 'World Wrestling Federation Superstars' performing on each track.

The single 'Slam Jam' achieved a creditable #4 in the UK singles charts, then music track 'WrestleMania' peaked at #14, while 'USA' featuring 'Hacksaw' Jim Duggan could only enter at #71.

It's safe to say the album did a lot more good than bad, and it gave wrestling more of a mainstream platform. Fun fact: Simon Cowell was the executive producer on the project.

Missing a trick from both WWF and WCW was the release of music theme tracks. *The Wrestling Album* was a 1987 release, but nothing would hit us in the UK until the *WrestleMania* album in 1993. With the talents of Jim Johnston, J. J. Maguire and Jimmy Hart (yes, the manager), wrestling theme music will live on to this day. Sadly not enough was provided in the early 1990s and it's only now, years later, that can we access the music library.

In 1994–95 pro wrestling faced uncertainty, viewership suffered, pay-per-view events didn't sell as expected and there was less general talk of wrestling. By 1995 many countries cancelled their TV deals with WWF as the interest had dwindled, and WCW suffered the same fate as their TV deal ended with ITV in this year. This all put wrestling in a precarious situation, a situation that could go either way.

Where did it all go wrong? Was wrestling finished? In reality, nothing was going wrong, and wrestling was certainly not finished. It was just the passage of time. Fans can only take so much of the same, which WWF and WCW knew, so new stars were being created. There are still some excellent parts to this period, it's just that a lot of it went unnoticed.

Rising from a tag team performer in the late 1980s to a main event headliner, Bret Hart did an exceptional job of forging the new generation of wrestling. He is adored today and remembered for his excellent wrestling skills.

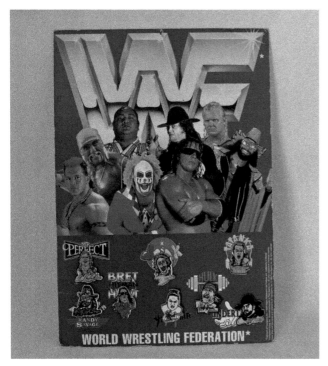

Released in 1993, these badges give you an idea of the cartoon characteristics WWF endorsed at that period. There are only eight badges from this set and, although they are seen as one here, they were available separately. It's uncertain if the badges were set for worldwide distribution, but they did have a feel of being a European exclusive.

Wrestling foams are the perfect item for live fan interaction. Many forms and variations of wrestling foams exist of wrestling superstars, ranging from your high-profile stars to the lower-end performers. Pictured here is the Chris 'Tatanka' Chavis axe-shaped foam and the Razor's Edge wrestling foam. It is important to check for condition when buying foams as many wrestling ones do not age well. Also, it's crucial to store them correctly if you are a collector.

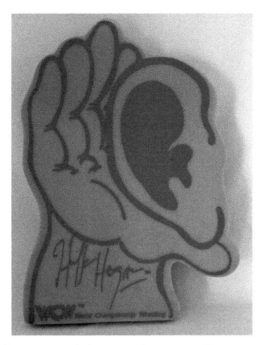

From 1994 this foam finger was made for WCW, featuring Hulk Hogan. The trademark cupped hand covers the ear, which was something only Hulk Hogan could gain recognition for. The major part to this piece is that there's a new sheriff in town. While filming *Thunder in Paradise* WCW quickly swooped on the signature of Terry 'Hulk Hogan' Bollea. Offering a better pay deal, Hulk Hogan would go on to change wrestling at WCW.

Don't forget the trusted wrestling annuals that continued to flood the market. This picture shows how WCW changed over the years. Notice the 'Surfer' Sting pictured to the top left and the latter 'Crow' Sting to the bottom right – it's hard to believe it's the same person.

Even though a void had been left when Hasbro cancelled the WWF deal, wrestling still marched on. A monthly dose of your favourite independent wrestling magazine filled you with inside knowledge and gave you hints as to what was coming next in the world of wrestling. As the internet was still in its infancy, other than word of mouth, magazines were the only place to go for wrestling news.

If you lived through the 1990s here's a taste of some of the fantastic independent wrestling magazines that stocked our newsagent shelves. *Powerslam*, *The Wrestler*, *Pro Wrestling Illustrated*, *Inside Wrestling*, *Wrestling Eye*, *Wrestling's Main Event* and *Wrestling Mania*. For good measure, pictured is a reminder of the ever-brilliant monthly *WCW Magazine*.

Hasbro abruptly ended its contract with the WWF sometime around late 1994/early 1995. It left a huge void in the merchandise market and fans felt frustrated as that meant no action figures to collect. Justoys stepped in and went on to produce the magnificent Bend-Ems range until 2001, consisting of fifteen variations of WWF wrestler series. Justoys would close their doors in 2004 after providing some excellent action figures for Star Wars, Disney, Marvel Comics, WWF and Hanna-Barbera to name a few.

Justoys gave WWF fans sixteen standard series, plus several extra added on bonuses. Many variations to the wrestling ring made it to stores, while all sorts of boxed sets and combined wrestling figures made up the toy line.

Pictured is the Series 4 action figures of Sunny and Marc Mero, plus the Power House seven-piece set from around the second series of release. Looking at the first Justoys image, you can see a Paul Bearer 'Ring Exclusive' was the prize pick; bizarrely, however, it wasn't quite exclusive as the action figure would soon become available later on in a separate series.

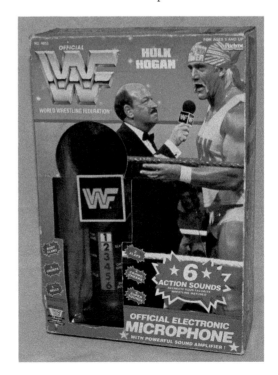

Out with the old and in with the new. By 1995 we start to see the shift in merchandise. Here is the vintage 1990 microphone, which featured six sound effects and the ultimate excuse to impersonate the late great 'Mean' Gene Okerlund. This has to be the ultimate roleplaying gadget of our time.

Jakks Pacific entered the toy universe in 1995 just as WWF was searching for their next business venture. With the stocking fillers of Justoys it didn't take long for Jakks Pacific and Titan Sports Inc. (WWE) to team together to embark on one of the highest-selling toy partnerships in history.

The partnership between Jakks Pacific and Titan Sports Inc. (WWE) lasted from 1995 to December 2009 and provided wrestling fans with a huge quantity of memorabilia. With a hot wrestling show and wrestling figures to match, Jakks Pacific would produce a huge number of various action figure lines, often selling in high numbers.

On the surface, 1995 looked tacky and off-paced, but in reality it was the start of brighter things to come. Pro wrestling had a hesitant vibe, but you could clearly see WWF, WCW and ECW were experimenting with new ideas. Come 1996 a rejuvenated wrestling era would kick-start the Attitude Era.

Sony launched a new games console – PlayStation – in late 1994/early 1995 and it quickly garnered interested, ultimately selling over 102 million units worldwide. Pictured here are just some of the fantastic wrestling games available for the PS1.

Here are two cameras: to the left is the WWF Slam Cam made in 1999 by MGI Software, and to the right is the retro 1991 Remco release of the Foto Wrestling Autofocus Camera made by Remco Toys.

A noticeable shift in wrestling from the early to late 1990s is WWF changing its focus from just one superstar. Hulk Hogan was heavily used to sell merchandise back then, but by the late 1990s images were mixed about in a more appealing way.

Entering the WWE in 1995 with the lame 'Ringmaster' gimmick, Steve Austin broke out as a superstar after winning the 1996 King of The Ring tournament. Using his famous quote 'Austin 3:16 just whipped your ass!' to a battered Jake Roberts, this turned Austin into wrestling's latest hot commodity.

Moving towards the Attitude Era of wrestling, it was Steve Austin who certainly got the ball rolling with his antics as wrestling's ultimate bad boy. Middle finger salutes, thug-like behaviour and attacks on WWE owner Vince McMahon actually made him one of the fan favourites in the company.

The 'Austin 3:16' brand meant big business for the WWE and it catapulted their revenue stream into the big league. Mass quantities of Austin merchandise filled the shelves, and he soon became the face of wrestling, overtaking the mantle left by Hulk Hogan.

With a new brand came new toys. There is no surprise that World Wrestling Federation would reach number 2 in the merchandise table come 1998, and Steve Austin had a dominant share on the sales side of things. Obviously, your Bret Harts, Undertakers and D-Generation X made an impact too, but Jakks Pacific and 'Stone Cold' Steve Austin dominated in the action figure world.

Steve Austin and the branded catchphrases that went alongside him – whether it be 'Stone Cold', '3:16', 'Broken Skulls Ranch' or the other smaller terms used – was hot property. Wherever you looked you couldn't move for his merchandise.

Starting off sluggishly, Jakks Pacific were hit and miss in many areas, but the company soon got their act together by 1997. Starting out in 1995 and lasting until 2009, Jakks Pacific's deal with the WWE saw them produce an enormous amount of wrestling merchandise; so much, in fact, it's hard to catalogue exactly what came from the factory.

Pictured here is the 'Action Ring' accompanied with wrestling figures and ringside accessories.

Never shy of capitalising, here are the three big stars of the Attitude Era. Action figures were often repackaged and refashioned. The wheels where always in motion and the Jakks Pacific/ WWE juggernaut didn't hold back. Plenty of variations exist of boxed-up action figures. This is just one showing off the 'Immortal Champions'.

Pictured here are some of the boxed WWF Jakks Pacific action figures from the late 1990s era of wrestling. The standard-sized action figure measured, on average, 6 inches high and are dissimilar to the WWF Hasbro range prior to this. All ranges and series of WWF/WWF Jakks Pacific action figures flooded the market, supplying the demand of hungry wrestling fans.

In their own unique way Jakks Pacific contributed greatly and maximised the alternative wrestling roster in a very positive spin. Collectors wanted managers, female wrestlers and more play accessories, so Jakks Pacific didn't hesitate in giving the fans what they wanted. In addition to the action figures, belts, ringside accessories, playsets and eventually a WWE Classics line propelled Jakks Pacific into the hall of fame category of toy makers.

This ginormous Insurrextion action figure set offers ten wrestlers and features the stars of the late 1990s/early 2000s. Insurrextion was an annual WWE pay-per-view event that ran from 2000 to 2003 and was produced exclusively for the UK audience. Jakks Pacific provided fans with all shapes and sizes of action figures and other crazy merchandise.

Jakks Pacific went on to produce miniature-sized action figures, and here is the King of The Ring playset. Other playsets of this type include Royal Rumble, Brawl-4-All, Buried Alive, WrestleMania, Survivor Series and Raw Is War, with many others known to exist.

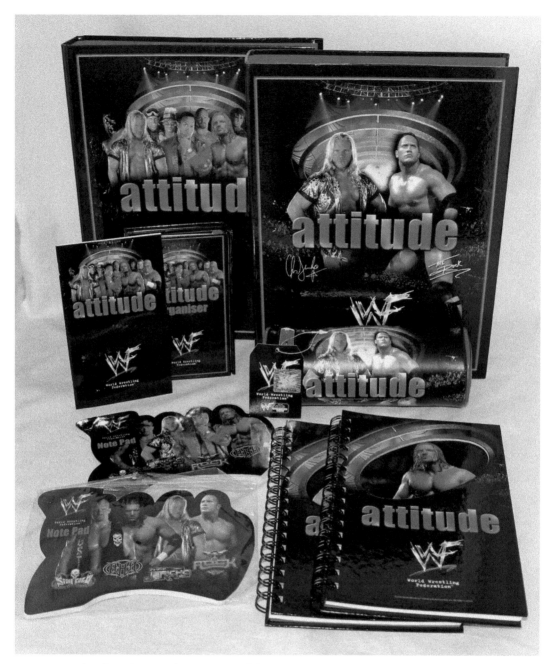

Depicted in the colours and impression of the 'Raw Is War' TV set, the Attitude stationary sets came with various frontal designs. Notice how WWE use a mixture of wrestling stars on these front covers – totally different from the early 1990s when Hulk Hogan took the prime spot.

   Raw Is War became WWE's flagship show, running from 1993 and providing over 1,000 weekly broadcasts. As the UK broadcasting lagged behind the USA, Sky Sports 3 would show the programme on Friday evenings at 10 p.m. What made things even better was TNT broadcasting *WCW Monday Nitro* from 9 p.m. on the same night.

Finishing the decade and *SmackDown!* enters the ring. Originally set out to be an all-women's wrestling show, *SmackDown!* would go on to prove popular with wrestling fans and it continues to be so to this day.

The stationary sets of the late 1990s pictured here are possibly the easiest items to find in the current climate. They are simply made and advertise the great Attitude Era of wrestling.

WCW endured three toy makers in its time: firstly Galoob between 1990 and 1991, then Original San Francisco Toy Makers (OSFTM) stepped in from 1994 to 1997, and finally it was Toy Biz, who contributed from 1999 until WCW's closure in 2001.

WCW Galoob had a major impact in the UK and went as far as including a UK-exclusive series, as mentioned earlier in the book. WCW Galoob action figures were the alternative to WWF's Hasbro toy line. WCW Galoobs were widely available and enjoyable to collect.

Original San Francisco Toy Makers operated longer than the WCW Galoob line, from 1994 to 1998, unlike previously the OSFTM toy line had two variant sizes: first the more popular 7-inch action figures, which emulated the WWF LJN toy line of the 1980s, and then secondly in 1997 came the 4-inch action figures, which matched up with the Galoob size. To add more confusion, 12-inch action figures became available in the United States.

One other thing to remember here is the availability of the action figures. The WCW Galoob line reached a modest number of retail stores, whereas OSFTM didn't have the same appeal. In all, OSFTM made some beautiful action figures, but sadly they were hard to find for the majority in the UK.

The third and final action figure line of WCW belonged to the more popular Toy Biz Inc. Kicking off in 1999, the WCW Toy Biz action figure line proved to be hugely popular and sold a good number of toys. Measuring around about the 6.5-inch mark, Toy Biz Inc. introduced collectors to an alternative wrestling figure, which came from their catchy series names. Smash N Slam, Slam And Crunch, Grip N Flip, Power Slam and TNT are memorable series from the WCW Toy Biz Line.

The Monday Nitro Arena pictured here was made by Toy Biz inc.

Two versions of the WCW toy championship belts are pictured here. The belt pictured closest was released in the early 1990s, and the one just behind hit stores in 1998. It's safe to say that the early 1990s wrestling belt is far superior. The 1998 version does have sound effects, but it's of poor quality. The microphone to the left was sold as a set with the belt, but that is also poor quality. There are no battery-operated sound effects, it operates of a spring coil and it's nothing to write home about.

WCW only released one style of wrestling belt in the late 1990s. WWF, on the other hand, had a larger number of replica toy belts on sale. WCW missed a trick there and should have upped production to four or five styles of wrestling belt.

Made by Toy Biz in 1999, this Ring Announcer series features Kevin Nash, Goldberg and a scarce 'Mean' Gene Okerlund action figure. It is one of many action figure products from the WCW Toy Biz line. With great detail on the action figures and fancy outer packaging to match, you can clearly see why the WCW Toy Biz line was so popular.

A WCW lunch box and drinking container depicting the three main players of the company. Like the WWF, by 1997 everything went from a vibrant colour to a Gothic-looking black.

When Hulk Hogan turned bad guy at WCW pay-per-view, Bash At The Beach 1996, he turned wrestling on its head and created shockwaves around the world. A hero to millions of kids and possessing a larger-than-life aura, nobody could believe that the Hulk could turn on fan favourite Randy Savage.

He now teamed with Kevin Nash and Scott Hall to create the newly formed faction the New World Order (NWO), and wrestling had to knuckle down and embrace the new attitude it brought with it. Hitting the buttons of the adolescent teens, wrestling had flipped from a family fun show to an edgier product. All of a sudden pro wrestling would mean big business again.

WCW created a fabulous storyline where the new faction of NWO had invaded its company, and a good number of wrestling fans actually believed the tale to be true. As more wrestlers joined the faction, the idea of WCW vs NWO turned into a reality. With a believable storyline like this, WCW were quids in.

As the NWO dominated the storylines and business plan, Bill Goldberg would soon force himself into the limelight as the number one star of WCW. Going undefeated for 173 matches, the whole world felt Goldberg was unstoppable. The streak drew the crowds in and everyone wanted a piece of the action.

The fresh, new approach of Bill Goldberg reignited the fire WCW had started. This photograph may indicate to you how popular his image carried. Bill Goldberg was the fresh face wrestling needed back in 1997.

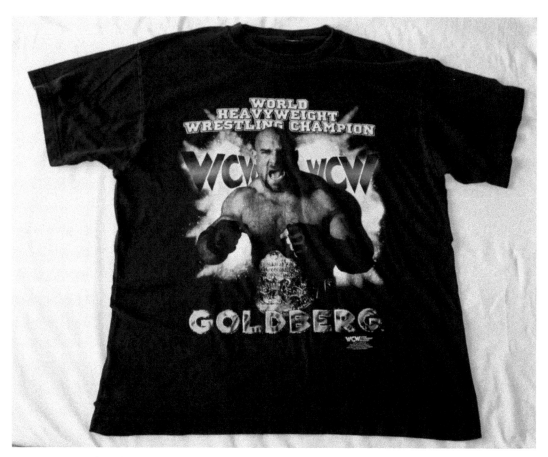

An original Goldberg T-shirt from 1998. The T-shirt highlights the fact he was World Heavyweight Champion. When Kevin Nash ended Goldberg's undefeated streak things weren't the same again for Goldberg no, it's safe to say, for WCW either.

By 1999 WCW was clearly a sinking ship. The drama had become a calamity, their top performers started dictating the pace and, above all, WWF began to gain momentum by producing incredible weekly TV shows. Goldberg's streak and impact on wrestling in unforgettable. Who knows, if WCW had kept the streak going a little longer they may still be in business today.

Pictured here is a sports bag with Goldberg and the WCW logo. Goldberg would rise high in the WCW ranks and soon become the poster boy for the company.

Not only did WCW have great wrestling shows, it's safe to say they beat the WWF hands down in the video game wars. THQ published several wrestling games for WCW, and the enjoyable gameplay put WCW at the top of the wrestling games list.

Handheld games such as those shown here continued into the late 1990s. In today's world this type of electronic game are next to non-existent as smartphones have largely taken them over. They are nice to look at as a nostalgia piece.

Made by Tiger in 1999, these four handheld electronic games include Diamon Dallas Page, Sting, Goldberg and Hollywood Hulk Hogan. If games weren't your thing, though, at least these 9-inch-high figurines look nice on display.

Like WWF, WCW had their fair share of absurd wrestling items. These four watches known simply as 'Wrestling Watch-It' hold a precious quartz analogue movement and were made by Allstar Marketing Group. The watches are probably of good quality, but realistically it's the ideal timepiece for a nurse. Wrestling fans have seen it all: from Smoking Gunns foam cowboy hats to talking soap, but someone out there must enjoy it.

WCW Slam Bam! Walkie Talkies featuring Goldberg and Sting. You can see that Sting is dressed in his 'Crow' ring attire, which was a drastic change from the 'Surfer' Sting attire he wore in the early 1990s. Something different from WCW, these walkie talkies have great caricature impressions.

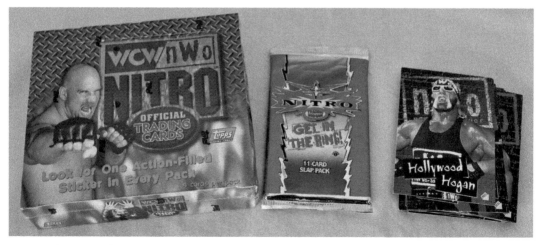

Made in 1999 by Topps cards, the sealed WCW/NWO Nitro cards are a rarity. Trading cards will always be fun to collect, and back in 1999 that was no different. The only regret here is wishing these were original Pokémon cards instead. They would certainly be of much higher value today!

The battles between World Championship Wrestling and the World Wrestling Federation continued on, with WWF eventually getting the upper hand towards the latter parts of 1998.

WCW would branch out internationally in 1999. This is something they had held back from for a number of years, which had given the WWF an advantage, especially as they held more pay-per-view events on UK soil.

One Night Only came live from the Birmingham NEC on 20 September 1997. Sky Sports offered a box office exclusive, enabling more UK wrestling fans to jump on board with the extravaganza. WWF followed up in 1998 with Mayhem in Manchester, which was again supported by box office and gave fans a piece of the action.

The UK wrestling scene started to grow and both companies knew the interest fans had in their brands. Although WCW never broadcast any pay-per-view events from the UK, they did at least tour the towns and cities again. WWE, as ever, struck when the iron was hot. Insurrextion, Rebellion and later Monday Night Raw all had the privileges of broadcasting live from the UK.

As the 'Monday night wars' continued, the merchandise followed. Pictured here are miniature finger skateboards, toy cars, key rings and key chains. The Goldberg car (pictured to the bottom right) is made of 24-kt gold. This is just a touch of the unusual merchandise from that era.

Carrying on with the catalogue and the WWF had bulked up their stock, increasing the volume of items available to purchase. Going with a darker, Gothic theme, the late 1990s era of wrestling merchandise was a success for the company and triggered mass sales. Merchandise became easier to find and retail outlets jumped on board, noticing the demand for wrestling products. If you weren't wearing a band T-shirt back in 1998 then it was either football or wrestling that substituted it.

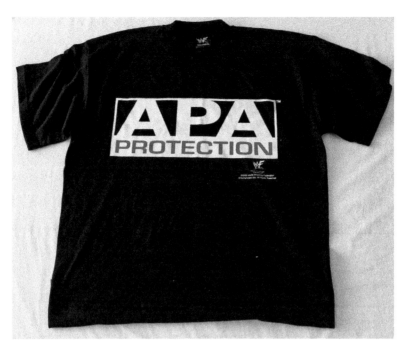

Gone were the multicoloured T-shirts and merchandise like we saw in the early part of the decade. In the later 1990s pretty much every T-shirt was black with a logo print over the front. In this example 'APA' is the initials of the tag team Acolytes Protection Agency, which consisted of Farooq (Ron Simmons) and Bradshaw (John Layfield) – a fun, no-nonsense tag team that fitted right in with the Attitude Era.

A wide range of mugs are pictured here that date back to 1999/2000 and show-off female wrestlers Trish Stratus and Lita. Chris Jericho and the Hardy Boyz even got their own wrestling mug. Plenty of alternatives were available, but it is nice to see female wrestlers being given more of a chance than they had in the past.

Unlike the earlier parts of the decade, in the late 1990s WWF and WCW begin to distribute their theme music, which became available on CD. CDs sold well here in markets including the USA and UK. Each wrestler had their own theme music and to hear it in the comfort of your own home was ideal.

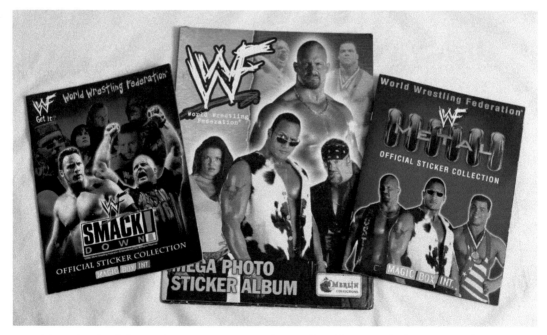

After a break of close to five years WWF wrestling sticker albums made their return. This time Magic Box International took over the realm and offered collectors a chance to complete the SmackDown! and the Metal sticker albums. A larger 'Mega Photo Sticker Album' by Merlin also became available in early 2001.

Dwayne 'The Rock' Johnson has become an acclaimed Hollywood movie star in modern times, but before that he started out as a wrestler (Rocky Maivia) way back in 1996 for the WWF. Going from your average mid-card wrestler to a high-earning superstar, like 'Stone Cold' Steve Austin he has left his mark on pro wrestling forever.

Known for his witty catchphrases and deeply engaging fan interaction, it's safe to say Hollywood was calling for this superstar. When many of Vince McMahon's top stars jumped ship to WCW in search of a bigger pay packet or an easier workload, McMahon's response was for the WWF to create newer, fresher superstars and The Rock was a prime example.

Super popular and becoming the face of the company, selling The Rock's merchandise never faltered. Simply fans couldn't get enough of their new hero. He's done well outside of wrestling too, starring in Hollywood blockbusters such as *Jumanji*, *Moana* and the *Fast and Furious* franchise.

Ever present and forever brilliant, the Undertaker was the reliable force behind the WWF's success. Played by Mark Calaway, the Undertaker debuted way back in 1990. After leaving a thirty-year legacy he retired at Survivor Series 2020.

From the old grey socks of Undertaker to the 'American badass' of the early 2000s, the character of the Deadman has regenerated itself in so many ways, keeping fresh and up to date with wrestling and everything surrounding it. Never one to throw in a lame performance, the Undertaker is a unique legend of pro wrestling.

Enduring the Golden Era, the Attitude Era, Ruthless Aggression Era and the present-day scene, the Undertaker's value to wrestling has remained the same – top class. The wrestling community adores the efforts of Mark Calaway and the merchandise is enough to fill many museums. Here is a brief glimpse of what came our way from the Undertaker.

Similar in design and size to the foam wrestling belts released in the early 1990s, Jakks Pacific introduced more championship belts. WWE often changed about their belt designs and in the late 1990s they introduced more wrestling titles. It was a clever move because with every belt redesign or new championship division came a whole new batch of toy merchandise belts. Look out for the sealed WWF belts because not many survive in the original packaging. Definitely a future collectible.

Sticking with the all-black T-shirt theme, this top is associated with the WrestleMania 2000 pay-per-view event. WrestleMania is wrestling's version of the Super Bowl or World Cup – the grandaddy of them all.

The money spinner of wrestling cards. Photographed here are just some of the wrestling cards, stickers and even transfer tattoos on offer from the late 1990s. After a lull in the mid-1990s, wrestling cards were back in force by the end of the decade.

Extreme Championship Wrestling (ECW) was one of those once in a lifetime experiences, and to truly appreciate the company you had to have lived through the era to fully appreciate the concept of the brand. Established in 1992 as Eastern Championship Wrestling, Tod Gordon, the then chairman, would expand ECW, captivating an audience intended for the more mature fan.

Extreme, hardcore wrestling matches featuring the use of barbed wire, sexual connotations, cigarette smoking and drinking alcohol gives you a feel for the target audience. By 1996 with the takeover by Paul Heyman, ECW would again up itself to the next level offering a great alternative to the two bigger companies of WWF and WCW.

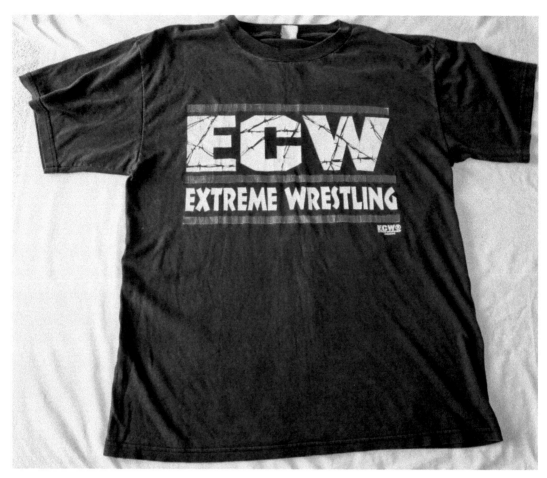

Unlike its rivals, ECW took a different approach to merchandise by targeting the bloodthirsty, hardcore wrestling fans. Afterall, ECW was intended for the eighteen-plus crowd. No flashy face paints or jigsaw puzzles were sold, just T-shirts or video tapes were available. Later they did branch out to DVDs and action figures, but that's about all.

Did you know that for ECW's mail order service, wrestlers often packed, labelled and shipped goods? It's hard to believe but it's true, and confirmed on the incredible *The Rise and Fall of ECW* documentary.

ECW was a wrestling organisation like no other. Many have tried to imitate it, but nothing can beat the original.

Stepping away from the norm, Original San Francisco Toy Makers (OSFTM) manufactured a range of ECW action figures in 1999 and 2000. With six series and forty-four action figures, the action figures are deemed a success among the wrestling community.

Having an action figure line for ECW was about the only thing the company branched out with. Everything else was aimed at the adult audience. This wasn't a poor effort of action figures either, OSFTM and ECW went the whole hog and gave the fans a wrestling ring and a ton of hardcore wrestling accessories – just how they'd want it.

Many wrestling fans know ECW operated on a shoestring budget, which left an open market for WCW and WWE to plunder its top talents on a regular basis. Pictured here is a WWF Dudley Boys '3D Death Drop' T-shirt – the former tag team champions of ECW.

Still, as this happened ECW struggled on, giving it their best shot by creating more great wrestling shows. With debts of close to £7 million, the original ECW brand closed its doors for the very last time in April 2001.

A resurgence in yo-yos made WWF and WCW act fast in producing the items here in question. Not quite the quality of the Coco-Cola or Pepsi-Cola yo-yos from years earlier, but still at least the effort had been made.

The four-pack of WWF yo-yos seen in the centre are average, standard yo-yos, but the Sable one lights up and plays theme music. WCW's version of the yo-yo had a ball bearing effect and, like the others, if you had the skills you could execute all sorts of tricks.

Released in 1999, this whacky game consisted of fifty-four magnetic coin medallions, and each were sold separately. The aim of the game is simple and fun to play. Attach string to the wrestler's head, place all magnetic coin medallions on the ground, then throw the wrestling heads towards the coin medallions. Whoever collected the most coin medallions won. This is fairly easy to obtain in North America and alternative head moulds are available.

Written across TV screens showing WWF, WCW and ECW was the popular slogan 'Do Not Try This At Home'. It's a prominent message even today and it's there to remind fans not to bother mirroring the efforts of the wrestling superstars. These fun, 4-foot inflatables went against the grain and, given a chance, any child would want to grapple them to ground, emulating The Rock or 'Stone Cold' Steve Austin.

Made by Artbox and distributed in 1999, it's safe to say that wrestling board games do not work, or at least as well as they should. For example the Wrestling Challenge game, which is complicated and hard to understand. The aim of the game is to choose a wrestler, collect four endorsement cards, then to roll a twenty-four-sided dice to determine the winner. This didn't fit in with the wrestling era at the time, and it's far from a classic.

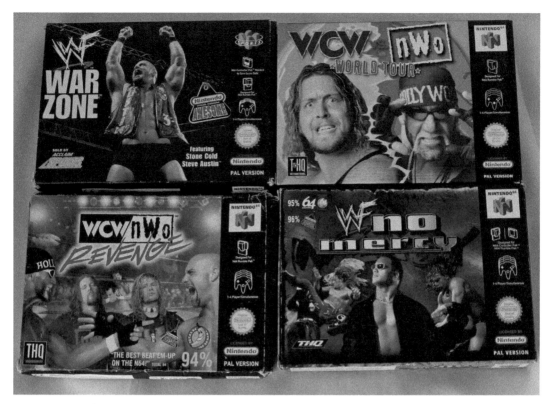

WCW made headway in video gaming thanks to the *WCW vs NWO World Tour* and *WCW/ NWO Revenge* releases. Developed by Asmik Ace Entertainment (AKI Corporation) then published by THQ, both games received rave reviews from the wrestling community and, above all, video gaming magazines. As WCW took poll position, *WWF War Zone* left fans frustrated and wanting more.

When THQ exited the contract with WCW, the tables would soon turn in favour of the WWF. Publishing great games like *SmackDown* and *SmackDown 2* for the PS1, the pairing of THQ and WWE released fantastic games together until THQ went bust in 2010.

WWF No Mercy is rated as the best wrestling game of its era thanks to Asmik Ace Entertainment and THQ.

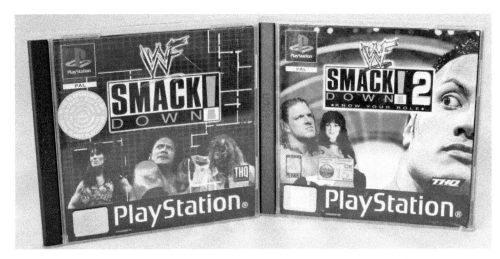

A revelation for the Sony PlayStation, after waiting a number of years finally a decent WWF wrestling game found its way to the console. Both *SmackDown!* and *SmackDown! 2 Know Your Role* had excellent gameplay, becoming popular with the masses. It's no surprise each game made it to platinum status on the Sony PlayStation console. (To achieve platinum status a game had to have sold over 400,000 copies worldwide.) Which was your favourite?

As the new millennium approached, VHS was steadily fading out and DVDs became the new replacement. Obviously, as DVDs had better visuals and a much improved sound quality, people wanted them. WWF got right on board and knew the direction things were going with the digital age that was on its way.

Even though they were a smaller-scale company, ECW understood the importance of technology and engulfed the change. But what is baffling is that WCW, owned by media mogul Ted Turner, never thought to take on the new age and strictly kept to VHS only. By 1999 WCW's home videos would be packaged and designed by world leaders Warner Bros, so goodness only knows why WCW never stepped into the DVD market.

Original WWF and ECW DVDs can fetch good money today. One thing to note is that nothing beats the original version.

Starting in 2004, the WWE Tagged Classics series were the perfect sentimental gift. Priced at £14.99, each DVD package included two wrestling events from years gone by. Silver Vision (distributors) offered the DVDs at an affordable price and kept to a strict scheme by releasing pay-per-view events together and not muddling the series up. After seven years and eighty-four series, the Region 2 exclusive DVD would stop in 2012.

Like the original WWF and ECW DVD versions, WWE Tagged Classics generate decent prices considering the majority of standard DVDs are worth next to nothing. The original WWF DVD *WrestleMania XVII* holds the most value and is a great addition to any collection.

A fine example of a wrestling jersey. Worn by many and adored by the majority, this jersey epitomised the attitude of its time. Explicit to say the least and displaying the infamous 'Suck It' label on the front, this certainly turned heads of many parents questioning if this was acceptable for a teenage wrestling fan. Life was very different in the 1990s and you simply couldn't get away with it today. It's a good job the number '69', which is on the reverse, is not pictured here then.

A truly iconic wrestling item. Expect to pay close to the £100 mark for an original DX WWF jersey today.

Recapping the glorious era of wrestling has been made easy thanks to the internet. Currently the WWE Network holds its entire back catalogue featuring the old weekly TV tapings, memorable pay-per-view events and all forms of documentaries and broadcasts. Vince McMahon, being the businessman he is, acquired all of the major competitors' video libraries along the way, making WWE the 'wrestling universe' of our childhood.

Holding the licences and image rights, World Wrestling Entertainment continues to provide wrestling fans with the nostalgic fix they need. Wrestling action figures featuring the stars of the past, documentaries on retired wrestlers, clothing with guys from the hall of fame, WWE really brings it home. Teaming with Mattel and Masters of The Universe (MOTU), WWE even managed to mix up a whole bunch of wrestlers and released a WWE Masters Of The Universe/WWE line in 2019.

Seeing as the market is already on track with the vintage era, the other option is to attend the meet and greets, wrestling conventions and one-off shows. It can be an overwhelming experience talking to a wrestling legend, but having those 1990s gems hand signed is a memory to last a lifetime.

Pictured here are hand-signed promo pictures. Some are greatly desired.

Vince McMahon would purchase World Championship Wrestling (WCW) from adversary Ted Turner in March 2001. Then, only weeks later, Paul Heyman and Extreme Championship Wrestling suffered the same fate, leaving the wrestling industry in a precarious position. A good portion of the wrestling talent, producers, ring crew and management were simply left without a job, or should we say a job on the scale they had once known. From wrestling in front of huge crowds and surviving on a fairly comfortable pay cheque, wrestlers now had to either work abroad in countries like Japan, Mexico and the UK or faced uncertainty wrestling on the smaller indie circuit elsewhere.

By June 2002 father and son Jerry and Jeff Jarett, plus help from friends, would open NWA: Total Nonstop Action Wrestling's doors for the very first time. They had a global audience and offered an alternative to the World Wrestling Entertainment (formerly World Wrestling Federation, WWF). Later shortened to just TNA (Total Nonstop Action), the company gained a steady reputation and in 2004 a suitable TV deal gave TNA a weekly slot airing nationwide in the States.

Building on Total Nonstop Action's success in 2005, Marvel Inc. produced a range of action figures, plus an international TV deal was struck and between 2005 and 2009 wrestling had a great alternative, which attract a huge fanbase.

Since the closure of the two big wrestling brands of WCW and ECW in 2001, wrestling has continued forward. Ring of Honor, a long stay in the business, started in 2002 around the same time as TNA Wrestling, producing quality wrestling shows week in, week out. They don't stand alone either, as more followed: Major League Wrestling, Dragon Gate Wrestling (Evolve), Pro Wrestling Guerrilla, National Wrestling Alliance and All Elite Wrestling have made a splash in the United States wrestling scene since.

British wrestling couldn't hold back as they wanted a piece of the action. Finally, after close to twenty-five years of competing under the doldrums and since *World of Sport (Wrestling)* was cut from ITV, the British wrestling scene slowly gathered a good form of credibility again. Frontier Wrestling Alliance, World Association of Wrestling and 1PW led the way. In time it would take for Insane Championship Wrestling, Preston City Wrestling and Progress Wrestling to continue the success and give British wrestling a much-deserved independent scene.

As Great Britain has and will forever be an innovator in the world of wrestling, it's safe to take a look back and give a mention to the exceptional talent that has arisen from these shores. Legends such as Kendo Nagasaki, Big Daddy and Giant Heystacks need no introduction as their era of wrestling opened pathways for the wrestling we love today. Davey Boy Smith, Tom Billington (Dynamite Kid), Darren Matthews (William Regal) and Mark 'Rollerball' Rocco, to name a few, held the fort as they conquered the globe, holding out against the world's biggest stars.

We can finish by saying 'thank you' to the continued success of the modern era wrestling performers such as Drew Galloway (McIntyre), Nick Aldis, Pete Dunne, Stu Bennett and the like. Also, we must mention the changing time of wrestling and how today the women's wrestling division has risen to be on par with the men's division. So let's not exclude the exceptional British female wrestling stars such as Paige (Saraya-Jade Bevis), Piper Niven (Kimberley Benson), Kayleigh Rae, Bea Priestley and Xia Brookside.

Upon finishing this book, one thing is for sure and that is wrestling and its memories will never die. The merchandise of yesterday is very much a part of the future and I do hope you've enjoyed taking this nostalgic look at how wrestling was for many of us in the 1990s.

Thank you for purchasing the book and reliving with me the golden times of wrestling.